The Art of Laziness

More from Library Mindset

100 Quotes That Will Change Your Life

100 Harsh Truths of Life

The Art of Laziness

Library Mindset

"One day you will wake up, and there won't be any more time to do the things you've always wanted. Do it now."

— Paulo Coelho

CONTENTS

Part 2: Tips & Techniques

INTRODUCTION

Two roads diverged in a yellow wood,
And sorry I could not travel both,
And be one traveler, long I stood,
And looked down one as far as I could,
To where it bent in the undergrowth;

Then took the other, as just as fair,
And having perhaps the better claim,
Because it was grassy and wanted wear;
Though as for that the passing there,
Had worn them really about the same,

And both that morning equally lay,

In leaves no step had trodden black.

Oh, I kept the first for another day!

Yet knowing how way leads on to way,

I doubted if I should ever come back.

I shall be telling this with a sigh,

Somewhere ages and ages hence:

Two roads diverged in a wood, and I—

I took the one less traveled by,

And that has made all the difference.

This beautiful poem by Robert Frost explains the power of the path that you choose. You can choose the easy path on which everyone is already walking or you can decide that you want to take the hard path. The truth is that most things you would like to have or achieve are never easy. They take time, effort, and focus. That's why choosing to take the hard path will make all the difference in your life.

As each moment unfolds before you, there are two paths: one is the road most traveled and the other is the one less explored. If you are striving to reach your goals and manifest your dreams, it's up to you to choose which path will lead you to them.

Life is short and if you're not careful, you will find yourself moving from A to B without any purpose. As the Roman philosopher Seneca said almost 2,000 years ago in a letter to his friend, Paulinus:

"It is not that we have a short space of time, but that we waste much of it. Life is long enough, and it has been given in sufficiently generous measure to allow the accomplishment of the very greatest things if the whole of it is well invested. But when it is squandered in luxury and carelessness, when it is devoted to no good end, forced at last by the ultimate necessity we perceive that it has passed away before we were aware that it was passing. So it is—the life we receive is not short, but we make it so, nor do we have any lack of it, but are wasteful of it."

I was watching an old interview with Jeff Bezos recently, in which he talked about a new kind of framework to make important decisions. Before starting Amazon, he used to work at an investment bank. One day, he told his boss that he wanted to leave his job to start selling books online (Amazon started by selling books online before they expanded into other categories). They went for a walk in Central Park in New York for about 2 hours and his boss said, "This actually sounds like a really good idea to me, but it would be an even better idea for somebody who didn't already have a job." He convinced Jeff Bezos to think about quitting for 48 hours before making a final decision. He then found a framework that helped him to decide. "Regret minimization framework". Basically, it means to minimize the number of regrets you have when you're old. Here is what Jeff Bezos said:

"I wanted to project myself forward to the age of 80 and say, 'OK, I'm looking back on my life. I want to minimize the number of regrets I have.' And I knew that when I was 80, I was not going to regret having tried

this. I was not going to regret trying to participate in this thing called the Internet that I thought was going to be a really big deal. I knew that if I failed, I wouldn't regret that. But I knew the one thing I might regret is not ever having tried. I knew that that would haunt me every day."

Imagine you're almost 80, looking back at things and wishing you did something differently. You will regret all the moments you wasted being lazy, sitting on a couch watching T.V. for no reason, spending hours each scrolling aimlessly through your social media feed with no purpose.

Think about this for a few minutes: what will you regret when you're 80 years old?

Here are a few regrets that you might have:

- Not doing what you love.
- Being lazy and wasting your time.
- Not spending more time with your family.
- Not taking care of your health.
- Working hard for nothing in return.

- Not traveling when you're young.
- Not enjoying your life to the fullest.

It's time to stop making excuses about why you can't do the things you want to do. Instead, start asking yourself questions about how you can do the things you want to do. It will force your mind to find a way. There is never a perfect time. The best time is always now.

WHAT IS PROCRASTINATION?

Procrastination comes from the Latin word *procrastinare*: "to postpone or delay."

It means to avoid doing what you need to do. As Seneca said,

"Putting things off is the biggest waste of life: it snatches away each day as it comes, and denies us the present by promising the future. The greatest obstacle to living is expectancy, which hangs upon tomorrow, and loses today. The whole future lies in uncertainty: live immediately."

We know very well what we should do but we don't do it. We delay doing things as long as possible. We want instant gratification, not long-term satisfaction.

The Enemy of Procrastination

The biggest enemy of procrastination is panic. As soon as the deadline gets near or there are huge consequences for you, that's when the panic sets in. Procrastination almost disappears in the face of panic. You suddenly get unlimited energy; you can work all night to finish your task but it's not a good way to live. If something is important you will get it done, even after procrastination, but the work will be mediocre. You will not reach your full potential.

Here is the problem with panic: it only arises when things become urgent. You don't panic if it's important but not urgent. You don't panic to learn a new skill. You don't panic when you read a book. You don't panic to spend more time with your family. These things are important but not urgent. You always tell yourself that you can do these things later. That's one of the drawbacks of procrastination – waiting for things to become urgent before you attend to them. The downside is that you hardly pay attention to the really important things in your life, such as spending time with family and friends or following your dreams.

The Paradox of Time

I learned this from the entrepreneur and influencer Sahil Bloom. Here is what's The Paradox of Time means:

We know time is valuable. We have been hearing this since our childhood. Everybody teaches you the importance of time and that you will never get it back, but our actions often show the complete opposite. We don't seem to care about time, thinking we have an endless supply of it. The concept of death is almost forgotten, and we think we have unlimited time with our family and friends. Unfortunately, we don't. We think we can always do the things that we want to do later but forget that time is running out.

With that realization, here are some of the key actions you should take to make use of your time:

Start doing the things you want to do.

Start spending time with the people you want to.

Learn the things you want to learn.

The clock is always ticking and with each passing second, time becomes more precious. Don't waste it!

Productivity Mask

Nobody wants to admit that they're lazy. We want to show the best version of ourselves to others so we wear a mask instead of doing the really important stuff. These are usually also the hardest, which is why we busy ourselves with unimportant things – things that don't improve our lives in any way. Sometimes, we do it deliberately but most of the time, we're doing it subconsciously. We spend a lot of time being engaged in tasks that are neither important nor urgent. This is even worse than simple procrastination. Instead of making progress, we simply go around in circles.

Here's what you need to do to break that bad habit:

Identify 3 things you did yesterday that were completely useless. Be conscious enough so that next time you're doing them, at least you will know that you're being lazy. Instead of doing important things, you're doing unimportant things, which is just another form of laziness.

Part 1

Mindset

"If you spend your time chasing butterflies, they'll fly away. But if you spend time making a beautiful garden, the butterflies will come.

Don't chase, attract."

LIFE IS SHORT

"You could leave life right now. Let that determine what you do and say and think."

– Marcus Aurelius

In ancient Rome, whenever a General came back after a victory, a ceremony was held in his honor. The victorious General would enter the City riding a chariot and people would gather in large numbers to celebrate their General's triumphs. Sitting in the chariot, right beside the general, sat a slave, whose sole responsibility was to whisper into the General's ear, *"Respice post te! Hominem te esse memento! Memento mori!"* It basically means, *"Look behind you! Remember that you are but a man! Remember that you'll die!"*

Here is an amazing quote from Steve Jobs' Commencement Speech in 2005:

"Remembering that I'll be dead soon is the most important tool I've ever encountered to help me make the big choices in life. Because almost everything — all external expectations, all pride, all fear of embarrassment or failure — these things just fall away in the face of death, leaving only what is truly important. Remembering that you are going to die is the best way I know to avoid the trap of thinking you have something to lose. You are already naked. There is no reason not to follow your heart."

Death Calendar

The image below is also known as the Memento Mori Calendar, with each circle representing one month of a person's life. It is based on the assumption that the average human lives around 80 years (if you are lucky). Whatever your current age is, let's say you're 30 years old, take a pen and fill in the circles until 30. With each new month that follows after that, fill in another circle. When you see the graphic representation of the years passing you by, it is a stark reminder that you need to make the most of every day of your life.

80 Year Human Life In Months

Here are the ages of some famous people on their deaths:

Tupac Shakur died when he was 25.

Alexander the Great died when he was 32.

Vincent van Gogh died when he was 37.

Martin Luther King Jr. died when he was 39.

Paul Walker died when he was 40.

Alan Turing died when he was 41.

Napoleon Bonaparte died when he was 51.

Julius Caesar died when he was 55.

Steve Jobs died when he was 56.

Marcus Aurelius died when he was 58.

Hannibal died when he was 64-66.

George S. Patton died when he was 60.

Marie Curie died when she was 66.

Nikola Tesla died when he was 86.

Pablo Picasso died when he was 91.

Life is short, sometimes much shorter than we think. We tend to assume we will live a long time before we die. Often, that's not the case. Our time on this planet is limited but our daily lives make us forget this.

Bearing that in mind, you need to ask yourself:

How can you be lazy?

How can you procrastinate?

Shouldn't life be about spending more time doing the things that we truly enjoy from the depths of our hearts? As Sahil Lavingia said, *"Procrastination is what happens when society has convinced you to desire something you don't really want."*

Do all the things you want to do as soon as possible because there is a chance that you will never get to do them if you wait too long.

If you want to travel the world, now is the best time. If you want to start a business, now is the best time.

If you want to go to the gym, now is the best time.

There has never been a better time than now to do whatever it is your heart desires.

You will thank yourself later.

100% RESPONSIBILITY

"The price of greatness is responsibility."

– *Winston Churchill*

A recent study by the psychologist Bas Verplanken and his team at Bath University revealed the top three New Year's resolutions people make each year:

1. Living healthier (23%)
2. Personal improvement or happiness (21%)
3. Losing weight (20%)

But 91% of the people fail to keep their resolutions. As Verplanken states, *"Many resolutions are made on*

December 31st, and go down the drain on January the 2nd."

And every time there is someone to blame.

The bottom line is that only you are responsible for your life. While you may be tempted to blame your friends, family, spouse, or anyone else for what you don't do, it's solely in your hands to take action. Although you may find some temporary relief in making excuses and convincing yourself it's out of your hands to do anything in this situation, that's not really true. There's always something that you can do, and you can always do your best. Every action that you take or don't take impacts your life and it's up to you to take control. So, the next time you blame someone else for your problem, consider the fact that you are relinquishing power and there will be consequences. In reality, your future is in the hands of your present actions.

Here is a beautiful Zen story:

Two men visit a Zen master. The first man says: “I'm thinking of moving to this town. What's it like?”

The Zen master asks: "What was your old town like?”

The first man responds: “It was dreadful. Everyone was hateful. I hated it.”

The Zen master says: “This town is very much the same.”

The first man leaves and the second man comes in.

The second man says: “I'm thinking of moving to this town. What's it like?”

The Zen master asks: “What was your old town like?”

The second man responds: “It was wonderful. Everyone was friendly and I was happy.”

The Zen master says: “This town is very much the same.”

Life is what we make it and reflects our actions to a large extent. If you don’t make the most of it by showing up and walking the talk, what do you expect will happen?

Nobody is coming to save you

Always remember:-

Nobody cares if you're lazy or not.

Nobody cares if you procrastinate or not.

No one can change your life. And, most importantly, nobody has any interest in changing your life. It's up to you to do it yourself. It's in your own hands. You procrastinate to your heart's content and wait for others to help, but you might be waiting forever. To get out of this mindset, begin by giving up on the idea that somebody else will come along and save you.

Harsh truths of life:

If you're lazy, that's a choice you make.

If you're unhappy, you can choose to be happy.

If you procrastinate, that's a bad habit you need to drop.

What are you going to gain by escaping from the responsibility of stepping up? In effect, nothing. If you want to change anything about your life, know that you are fully responsible for doing so. Although complaining is easy enough, it achieves nothing. You need to act. You can start today, or you can wait till tomorrow. The choice is yours.

"The best time to plant a tree was 20 years ago. The second-best time is now."
— Chinese Proverb

Mistakes aren't as bad as you think

It's okay to make mistakes. They are a natural part of life and it's normal to screw up now and again. Since you are responsible for your actions, see mistakes as a lesson and move on. Learn from them and make a commitment to yourself to do better next time. Even if you are afraid of tripping up, it's better to experience that than to succumb to inertia. Jumping into the unknown can be scary, but it's the only way to move forward.

If a mistake happens, learn from it and move on. Rather than stagnating in a pool of apathy and procrastination, swim down the river and get into the flow of life. As the well-known adage says, if you ain't moving, you ain't living!

"Success does not consist in never making mistakes but in never making the same one a second time." — George Bernard Shaw

Focus on yourself

Don't worry about things that aren't your concern.

If something doesn't affect you, why get distracted by it?

People are constantly worrying about things they can't control, such as the opinions of others, even what complete strangers think of them. This can trap you in a mindset of self-doubt, blocking you from really flourishing as a unique individual. Instead, keep yourself focused on what truly concerns you and stop worrying about the opinions of others. You can't change them and will waste far too much energy that you could put to better use. Focus on yourself and what is important to you.

"Keep your attention focused entirely on what is truly your concern and be clear that what belongs to others is their business and none of yours."
— Epictetus

The 3 types of people:

In general, we can say that there are 3 types of people:

1. The first one is the majority of people. They never start what they would like to do and end up doing nothing at all. They never work on their dreams. They never do what they are supposed to do. They are just waiting around for something good to happen.

2. The second type of people are those who start something but never finish it. As soon as things get tough, they give up, and then spend the rest of their time regretting it.

3. The third type of people are those who work hard, don't give up despite hardships, and keep going. They are the one percent who do become successful.

One thing this third type of people have is persistence. Even when things don't run smoothly, they persevere with an end goal in sight. Things can go and will go wrong in life–that's just how it is. Your path will be full of obstacles but as long as you keep going, you can progress toward your goals.

Life is not a sprint but a marathon. It's long and hard, requiring stamina, strength, and persistence. There is no prize for quitting halfway but the sense of achievement you will feel when you achieve your goals is the best reward there is.

SURROUND YOURSELF WITH THE RIGHT PEOPLE

"You are the average of the five persons you spend the most time with." — *Jim Rohn*

In 2001, Warren Buffett posed a crucial question to students at the University of Georgia. He presented a scenario where you could view an individual as a company and potentially invest in them. Under this scenario, you would receive 10% of their future income (which could also extend to their health, happiness, or knowledge).

Who would you pick? And why?

The question is, what do they do differently from you? What habits have they adopted that you don't have?

This also works the other way around. If you have to reduce a person's income:

Who would you pick? And why?

Many of us choose to surround ourselves with people who have the same expectations as ourselves, the same goals, and the same level of motivation. If those people have few expectations, don't have any clear goals, and lack motivation, we will probably feel the same.

If your friends are lazy, then you'll probably also be lazy.

If your friends procrastinate, you are also more likely to procrastinate.

On the other hand, if your friends work hard, you'll also probably work hard.

If your friends read books, you are also more likely to start reading books.

There may be an outlier, but that's very rare. The main reason people stagnate is because whoever they spend most of their time with is also inactive. Basically, you adopt the habits of the person who is the closest to you. Their good or bad habits become yours. If your friend likes to waste time, you'll also join him in wasting time. It's easy enough to be influenced by others, especially those in your close circle. This also works the other way around. If you have friends who are always on the go, working toward their goals and have adopted good habits, that will rub off on you.

The choice is yours. The people you surround yourself with have a massive impact on your life. They shape your thoughts, actions, and your future. The right people can distinctly improve your life and the wrong ones will only worsen your life.

Change Your Circle to Change Your Thinking

If you want to change your thoughts, you must change everything you do. That includes changing the people you hang around with. If your buddies, pals, or close acquaintances are lazy, negative, and not making a positive impact on your life, it may be worth changing your circle of friends or, at least, not listening to their advice.

Someone once said:

"Surround yourself with people who have dreams, desire, and ambition; they'll help you push for and realize your own."

Don't Take Advice from Everyone

Don't take advice from someone you wouldn't wish to change places with. Let's say you want advice on how to be happier; the last person you should ask is someone who is always miserable. Think about it: if their advice had any value, why aren't they happy themselves?

Who you take advice from will decide the life you're going to live.

- Take advice from unhappy people, and you will become unhappy.
- Take advice from unhealthy people, and you will become an unhealthy person.
- Take advice from angry people, and you will become angry.

"If they don't have what you want, don't listen to what they say." — Alex Hormozi

Diderot Effect

Around 250 Years ago, the French philosopher Denis Diderot was quite well-known but despite his popularity, he was poor. His daughter was planning on getting married but he didn't have the money to give her a dowry. When Catherine the Great, Empress of Russia, heard about his predicament, she offered to buy the Diderot library. Suddenly, the philosopher found himself with a lot of money. He replaced his old robe with a new scarlet robe. Although he loved the robe, he realized that the other things he owned weren't as beautiful. His shoes didn't match the beauty of the robe and, in a short time, he bought new leather shoes, a wooden desk to write, a golden clock, and many works of art. All these expenses eventually led to him ending up in debt. This kind of behavior is now known as the Diderot Effect.

This same principle applies to your actions. The Diderot Effect can relate to accumulating bad habits in a similar way to accumulating material possessions. Just as obtaining a new possession can lead to a spiral of consumption, acquiring a new bad habit can lead to a spiral of negative behavior.

For example, if you pick up the habit of smoking cigarettes, it may trigger a desire for other behaviors that complement smoking, such as drinking alcohol excessively or engaging in unhealthy eating habits. This cycle of reinforcement can perpetuate the development of additional bad habits, creating a downward spiral of negative behaviors.

Similarly, just as the Diderot Effect involves a disruption of one's self-image, leading to a desire for harmonization with the new possession, acquiring a bad habit can disrupt your self-concept and lead to a desire for behaviors that align with the new habit, even if those behaviors are detrimental.

Overall, the Diderot Effect is a useful analogy for understanding how one negative behavior can lead to the accumulation of additional bad habits over time.

YOUR COMFORT ZONE IS YOUR ENEMY

"A comfort zone is a beautiful place, but nothing ever grows there." — Unknown

One of the biggest reasons people are lazy and put everything off until tomorrow is because they get too comfortable with their lives. You may not wish to change the way things are going because it's too much of an effort to do otherwise. That's an easy option but it doesn't lead to the growth that you want.

Growth demands that you step out of your comfort zone and do the hard things. It's easy to spend all your free time watching movies and scrolling through your social media feed all day but that's not meaningful. Your body and your brain know you're wasting your time. That's why you feel so bad after spending time doing nothing, instead of being engaged in something meaningful. The lethargy you experience drains you of the inclination to get up and start actively engaging in life. When this happens, nothing is going to change automatically. You need to push past that cozy comfort zone inertia and start to make things happen. After leaving their comfort zone, nobody says that they wish they stayed there.

Keep it simple!

Whenever you're trying to attempt something new, try to keep it as simple as possible. Trying to do too much can have a boomerang effect, bringing you back to earth with a thud. The less complicated you keep things, the better. Obsessing about all the things that can go wrong will also backfire, leading you to retreat into doing nothing. Most of the time, things don't go as badly as you may think but you won't know that until you give it a go. What you should do is start as soon as possible. You need to have a sense of urgency and the urge to do things quickly. Not the kind of urgency to achieve the desired results but the urgency to actually do the work. Let's say, for instance, that you want to learn how to create a website. You can start right now, or you can keep putting it off.

Even if your first plan doesn't go exactly as you had expected, that's okay. Just keep making adjustments and if you need to change your plan altogether, take a flexible approach. Do whatever it is you wish to do as soon as possible. Speed is crucial because you don't have as much time as you think. Keep things simple and do them with lightning speed.

"Most decisions should probably be made with somewhere around 70 percent of the information you wish you had...if you wait for 90 percent, in most cases, you're probably being slow." — Jeff Bezos

Start to think a little bit differently!

"If everyone is thinking alike, then somebody isn't thinking." - George S. Patton

You do not need to think just like everyone else or follow the crows. You can judge for yourself. You can think like no one else, and that's what makes you unique

In fact, by thinking differently and doing things differently from everyone else, you will get different results. If you do what everybody else is doing, you will only get the same results. Neither should you keep doing what you have been doing in the past and expect a different outcome this time. The end result is likely to be the same as before. If, for example, you sit on your couch all day complaining about your lot, you know what the result of that will be, right?

Parkinson's Law

This law was introduced by the writer and naval historian, Cyril Northcote Parkinson. Basically, the law states that work expands to fill the time allotted for completion. So, if you allow yourself 2 hours to finish a task, it will take 2 hours but if you only have 1 hour, you will find a way to complete the task in an hour. If you cannot start a project or it takes too long to complete, understanding Parkinson's Law can aid in overcoming procrastination. Setting shorter deadlines creates urgency and motivates action. With less time available, you are more likely to become more focused and efficient, breaking tasks into manageable chunks and prioritizing effectively. By recognizing that work expands to fill the time allotted, you can harness this principle to combat procrastination tendencies and make sure that important tasks are completed efficiently within tight time frames.

Set clear goals

It's important to set clear goals that are both possible and can be achieved quickly. Setting huge, ambitious goals isn't bad but the problem is, if you're a super lazy person, you won't work toward that goal because it would seem too hard and impossible to achieve.

That's why, at the start, you should set small, easy goals that can be achieved.

Goals should also be clear. For example, a clear goal is that you want to lose 2 kilograms in 1 month. An unclear goal is that you want to lose weight.

A goal that can't be measured and has no time duration is not a goal. It's like expecting a miracle to happen.

Write down your goals

It's a good idea to write down your goals on paper and if you don't usually do so, now is the time to start. When you have clearly written goals and read them regularly, they will help to motivate you. You may experience some pangs of guilt if you don't do what you have written down so it is a useful habit to adopt. Even if you only achieve half of your goals, that's still better than nothing.

Don't overcomplicate things

I'm not a big fan of all the various apps people use to measure their productivity. Although some people may find them helpful, you don't need any app to focus on your goals. All you need are two things: a pen and paper. That's it. Why overcomplicate simple stuff? Spending so much time on apps can actually be a waste of time and there's nothing more effective than good old-fashioned writing. All you have to do is list the following:

What you want to achieve.

How you can go about achieving it.

What timescale you set yourself.

How you can measure your progress.

How realistic your goal is.

Think long-term

There are two ways to approach life. You can think long-term and do the things that will be valuable for you in the years to come or you can satisfy your short-term pleasures and ignore the future.

It's crucial to bear in mind that the actions you take in the present are going to affect you later on in life. One thing that I can tell you for sure is that you will always regret being lazy. Laziness feels good in the present as it gives an immediate dopamine hit. Doing something new is hard and doesn't have that instant kick but as the years pass by, you will always regret not doing the things you wanted to do.

We live in a society where instant gratification has become the norm. Everyone wants everything and they want it now! While that may be okay in some respects, the reality is that striving to achieve anything of value takes time and effort. That might involve a fair amount of stress and a few sacrifices along the way but it's worth it if you want to achieve your future goals.

I'm not saying avoid all the fun in the present but, sometimes, it's necessary to make small sacrifices to secure a better future.

Take Risks

Don't be afraid of taking risks. If you want to achieve anything in your life, you must jump from a comfortable position to an uncomfortable one. The regret of not taking a risk later on in life can weigh heavily on you, especially as there is no going back.

"The biggest risk is not taking any risk... In a world that is changing really quickly, the only strategy that is guaranteed to fail is not taking risks." — Mark Zuckerberg

No Good, No Bad

It's a good idea not to fall into the trap of thinking that whatever happens to you is either good or bad.

Personally speaking, a lot of bad things have happened to me and I'm happy now that they did because they changed the trajectory of my life. Here's a great story to exemplify that:

There was a farmer with a horse that helped him in the fields. The villagers constantly told the farmer how lucky he was to have such a great horse.

"Maybe," he would reply.

One day, the horse ran away. The villagers came to the farmer to express their sympathies.

"That's too bad." the villagers said.

"Maybe," the farmer replied.

A few days later, the horse returned home with ten strong wild horses.

"That's great, isn't it?" the villagers said.

"Maybe," the farmer again replied.

The next day, the farmer's son was riding one of the horses when he fell off and broke his leg.

The villagers arrived to express their dismay.

"That's too bad," they said.

“Maybe,” the farmer replied.

A military officer marched into the village the next day, recruiting able-bodied young men for the war. The farmer’s son, with his broken leg, was left behind.

The villagers were joyful, “Your son has been spared. What fantastic luck!”

The farmer smiled.

“Maybe.”

DO THE HARD THING FIRST

"The cold water doesn't get warmer if you jump late."
— Unknown

Our mind has a tendency to opt for the easy options. That's why we need to be conscious enough to choose the best option, no matter how difficult it may seem. That may be hard to do when all we wish for is to relax, zone out, or put things off until another day. Let's face it, who wants to make life difficult for themselves? For example:

- It's easier to sit on the couch and watch TV than go for a run.
- It's easier to scroll on social media than to read a book.
- It's easier to procrastinate than to work hard.

Despite what you may be inclined to do, the hardest work you have for the entire day should be done first. No matter how challenging it seems, it needs to be done first. Only when you have completed it should you allow yourself to do the easy stuff or nothing at all. One way to achieve this is to make a list of all the things you have to do on any given day. Then, pick the hardest and most complicated task, and start it immediately. This task is the most important and, although we humans don't like to be uncomfortable, some things need to be done, no matter how testing they are.

Hard Choices = Easy Life

We all want to live an easy life with no worries; a life where we don't have to do anything we would prefer not to. Who doesn't want a life like this–one of complete freedom to do anything they like and not have to force themselves to go through difficulties?

The truth is, that if you want to have an easy life, you need to make hard choices. There is no reward in life in opting for the easy options. You will only be rewarded for the hard things you can do. Anyone can take the easy route but it's the hard one that pays off. There is no other way.

Easy Choices = Hard Life

Hard Choices = Easy Life

This is a harsh fact of life and the choice is yours: make those hard choices to live an easy life or go for the easy choices and live a hard life.

Whenever you're feeling lazy and don't feel like doing the work, think about your future self. Ask yourself where you would like to be in 5, 10, or 20 years. However you envisage your future, remember that it starts now, here in the present. The actions you take today will shape how your future is going to look.

"People do not decide their futures; they decide their habits, and their habits decide their futures." — F. M. Alexander

THIS TOO SHALL PASS

Once, a king called upon all of his wise men and asked them, 'Is there a mantra or suggestion that works in every situation, circumstance, place, and time? In every joy, every sorrow, every defeat, and every victory? One answer for all questions?'

The wise men were puzzled by the king's question. One of them, an old man, suggested something that appealed to all of them. They approached the king and handed him something written on a piece of paper. He had to promise not to read it, except under circumstances where he might find himself alone and there seems to be no way out. The king folded up the paper and placed it inside his diamond ring.

Sometime later, neighboring warriors attacked the kingdom. The king and his army fought bravely but lost the battle, forcing the king to flee on his horse. The enemies were in hot pursuit, getting closer and closer. Suddenly, the king found himself arriving at a dead end with nowhere to go. Below him was a rocky chasm, a thousand feet deep. If he jumped into it, he would be finished. Unable to do a U-turn and with the sound of enemy horses fast approaching, the king was desperate. There seemed to be no way out.

Just then, he saw the diamond in his ring glinting in the sun and remembered the message hidden within it. He opened the diamond and read what the note said: THIS TOO SHALL PASS.

The King read it again and again. Suddenly, something struck him. Yes! This too will pass. Only a few days ago, I was enjoying my kingdom. I was the mightiest of all the kings. Yet today, the kingdom and all my pleasures have gone. I am here trying to escape from my enemies. Just as those days of luxuries have gone, so too will this day of danger. A calm came over him and he simply stood there, without fear or desperation. The spot where he stood was full of natural beauty and it occurred to him that he had never known such a beautiful place existed in his kingdom.

The revelation of the message had a profound effect on him. He forgot all about his pursuers and, after a few moments, realized that the clacking of the horses' hooves was receding. His enemies had ridden off into another part of the mountains and were nowhere to be seen.

The king immediately regrouped his army and fought back with even greater bravery than ever before. He successfully defeated the enemy and regained his kingdom. On his return, he was received with much fanfare. The whole capital rejoiced in the triumph of their great king and his army.

His subjects were in a festive mood, showering flowers on their monarch from every house and street corner. People danced and sang, celebrating the vanquished king. The king, flattered by the praise, proudly said, "I am one of the bravest and greatest kings ever to have lived. No one can defeat me.' At that moment, the diamond in his ring glinted again in the sunlight, reminding him of the message. He opened it and reread it:

THIS TOO SHALL PASS.

The story teaches us a valuable lesson about facing life's ups and downs with resilience and perspective. No matter how tough things may seem, it's essential to remember that circumstances change. By embracing the idea that "this too shall pass," we can find the strength to endure hardships and even remain humble in times of success. This mindset encourages us to focus on inner resilience rather than worrying about failure. Ultimately, it empowers us to navigate life's challenges with courage, knowing that brighter days lie ahead.

WORK ON THE RIGHT THINGS

"Even Michelangelo would have trouble getting out of bed if he had nothing but a day of spreadsheets ahead. It's hard to imagine Leonardo da Vinci working for a corporation or being a government bureaucrat." — Vizi Andrew

It's very important to ask yourself if you are working on the right thing.

You will always be reluctant if you don't love what you do and pursuing a task without putting your heart and soul into it isn't going to make you feel good. Even your body will start telling you it's time to change your job. If you feel lethargic, exhausted, sick, or burnt out, it's probably because you don't find any meaning in what you do. It's never easy to be motivated by things that hold no meaning to you.

If your work is repetitive, boring, uninspiring, or meaningless, it's going to be very hard for you to feel happy about your life.

Remember that no job is more important than living a fulfilled life. Although there may be times when doing what you love is hard, it will still bring you more satisfaction than any easy, boring 9-5 occupation.

It's important to follow your passions because, by doing so, you will find yourself working with immense enthusiasm and contentment. It's no use becoming an accountant, for example, if your passion is to paint. At some point in the future, you will eventually feel disillusioned and unfulfilled.

Work is happiness

You'll probably spend most of your life doing some kind of work. If you don't choose what you want, somebody else will choose it for you, and you may not like it. If your parents coax you into studying law when you would prefer to be a gardener, your future career will always feel like a burden to you. But if you choose a career that aligns with your inner passions, you will be blissful. Your job is the pathway to happiness. You can't be happy if you don't like your job. You can never be motivated to work if you don't like your job. On the other hand, If you love your job, you will never feel lazy about doing it. You will even forget the concept of laziness entirely.

I have one piece of advice for you: if you don't love what you do, start finding a way to leave as soon as possible. Look for something that ignites your passion and aligns with your goals. It will make you at ease with existence.

Listen to your inner self; it will guide you.

Don't run away from hard things

Doing what you love doesn't mean running away from the complex aspects of your job. Neither does it mean you give anything less than 100% or that you become complacent.

Usually, whenever we start doing something new, we are highly motivated and begin in earnest. Once that initial motivation wears off, reality sets in and the challenges begin to surface. This is where problems can arise, with every task seeming more challenging, and it's at this point we start disliking our job. Even if it is our passion, we may be faced with hurdles we need to overcome. Needless to say, following your passion doesn't guarantee that you will always be happy.

When Vincent Van Gogh was 27, he dedicated himself entirely to painting. He used to work with extreme intensity. Painting was his whole life and he was highly productive. He used to paint at lightning speed but despite his hard work and genius, he struggled financially because his painting wouldn't sell. He was a man ahead of his time.

His younger brother, Theo Van Gogh, had to support him financially. Later on in life, Vincet's mental health deteriorated and on July $27^{th,}$ 1890, he shot himself in the chest with a pistol while painting alone in a field. He died two days later.

Van Gogh's tragic end highlights the toll that pursuing one's passion can sometimes take. It's a poignant reminder that passion alone doesn't guarantee happiness or success. We must also be prepared to confront and overcome challenges in the pursuit of our dreams.

Ultimately, we need to cultivate courage and perseverance, understanding that overcoming obstacles is often part of the journey toward fulfillment and self-realization.

Learn to prioritize

You can't do everything. Just like everyone else. you have limited energy and should spend it in the best way possible. If you spread yourself too thinly, you risk exhaustion and no results. That's the point at which you are more likely to give up, seeing little reward for all of your efforts. It's much more productive to focus your energy on selected tasks. In this case, less is definitely more.

Attract, don't chase

Another useful lesson in life is not to chase after everything. Instead, work on making yourself better so that you attract whatever it is you seek. By focusing on yourself, everything will fall into place.

You are great!

You may have told yourself that you aren't good enough to achieve your dreams. This kind of negative self-talk is a habit that can be broken. Instead of being your own worst enemy, start giving yourself a pep talk. You can do whatever you want once you put your mind to it. Rather than down-talking yourself, tell yourself how good you are at specific things and raise your self-confidence. One of the main reasons why people remain lazy is that they tell themselves they aren't good enough. Start telling yourself you are great and believe it!

DON'T BE A PERFECTIONIST

"Perfectionism is a disease. Procrastination is a disease. ACTION is the cure." — Richie Norton

I'm not saying that perfection is necessarily a bad thing, but it's impossible to be perfect in every aspect of your life. Beautiful things exist because someone spends a lot of time on tiny details. Without perfection, the world wouldn't be that great. But beauty also lies in imperfection. Just think of the Mona Lisa and I am sure you get my meaning. The world is beautiful both due to its perfection and imperfection.

Leonardo da Vinci was obsessed with tiny details. He would spend years trying to paint a single painting. When designing the Cathedral of Milan, he created hundreds of designs. It took him more than ten years to paint his most famous masterpiece, the Mona Lisa. I doubt very much, though, that Leonardo was perfect in other areas of his life.

Steve Jobs also had a crazy obsession with details. When designing the first Macintosh computer, he insisted that the circuit board wires should look straight and beautiful even though no one would see the inside as only the technician could open the computer with special tools. Was his obsession worth the time and energy? For him, definitely.

If you're painting or creating something that means a lot to you, then yes, you want it to be as perfect as possible. But if you're doing something mundane like cutting grass, which is only going to regrow in a few weeks, is it worth spending your entire day trying to cut each blade of grass to perfection?

My point is that you don't need to be perfect at everything and should be able to turn on and off the perfectionism switch. Sometimes it's needed, and other times it's not. Instead of having a default setting of always being a perfectionist, change it according to the circumstances. This will help you to throw all of your energy into the things that mean the most to you and still be able to finish other less interesting tasks instead of procrastinating about doing them.

Here is an excellent quote by Robert Schuller:

"Better to do something imperfectly than to do nothing flawlessly."

Done is better than perfect

Not all things can be done perfectly so there is no point spending days on a task that can be done in a few minutes. There is a difference between getting a job done satisfactorily and striving for perfection with every task. A job done well is better than a job not done at all because you are stressing out about every fine detail. If you constantly worry about doing everything to perfection, you may get so overwhelmed by the details that you are put off before you even get started.

DON'T BE MEDIOCRE!

"Mediocrity doesn't just happen. It's chosen over time through small choices day by day."

– Todd Henry

We always have the choice of becoming great or becoming mediocre. To become great isn't an easy task. You must give your very best each day. There will be failures. You will struggle a lot. To become mediocre, you don't have to do anything; your goal in life is to be an average person. Mediocre people never give their best; they settle for things being just okay because they know that anything else will be too difficult.

99% of people most likely settle for less than they want. They settle for jobs they hate and then wonder why they aren't productive, lack motivation, and don't wake up with the energy needed to do their job.

How can you wake up happy doing something you hate?

"Your work will fill a large part of your life, and the only way to be truly satisfied is to do what you believe is great work. And the only way to do great work is to love what you do. If you haven't found it yet, keep looking. Don't settle. As with all matters of the heart, you'll know when you find it."

– Steve Jobs

Nobody really wants to be mediocre. If you don't believe it, ask someone, "Do you want to become mediocre?" The answer is always going to be, "No."

The one big reason people settle for being mediocre is that everyone around them is also mediocre. If you try to become a little bit ambitious around these kinds of people, they will tell you all sorts of things to sabotage your ambition. They don't want you to shine because that will make them look dull. Internally, they could feel bad, feeling they have wasted their own potential.

When we are children, we have all sorts of dreams and aspirations. As we grow up, something happens and we all fall in love with mediocrity.

When you lose that sense of drive inside you to achieve something, time passes by, leaving you dragging your feet through life instead of living it.

Think big!

Even if you fail, that will still be better than the regret of never trying to push your boundaries. Imagine being an 80-year-old, wishing you could travel the world, pursue your dreams, and live how you want to, not how other people want to.

You still have time. At least for now. One day, there will be no time to do anything. Death will be standing at your door.

That's why it's important to always live your life doing what you want. You won't need any incentives or productivity tips; you will stop being lazy because a sense of purpose will take hold of you.

- If you don't like your job, change it.
- If you don't like your friends, change them.

- If you don't like your way of thinking, change it.
- If you don't like your life, change it.

Remember that a life of greatness is harder than a life of mediocrity. It's not easy, but the path will be worth it.

THE MYTH OF MULTITASKING

"The man who chases two rabbits catches neither."
— Confucius

On December 11, 1998, NASA launched the Mars Climate Orbiter to study the climate of Mars. It cost $125 million to build. On September 23, 1999, the craft entered orbit with Mars, and then suddenly, NASA lost contact with it. It was due to a simple error: engineers had failed to convert from English units to metric. The spacecraft got too close to Mars and was destroyed.

The example illustrates the potential disadvantages of multitasking, particularly in situations where precision and attention to detail are crucial. In this case, the engineers responsible for the mission were likely juggling multiple tasks and responsibilities, leading to oversight and error.

Multitasking means doing more than one thing at a time. It sounds good but it doesn't always work. When we focus on multiple important things at once, something has to give. Trying to focus on two important tasks at the same time can reduce your efficiency and stop you from completing either successfully. You're also more likely to tire quickly if you switch tasks continuously.

As the saying goes, *"The devil is in the details."* You need to have complete focus on whatever you're doing at the moment. The more you switch from one task to another, the less productive you will be and when you're tired, you're less likely to pay attention to tiny details.

The best thing you can do to improve your productivity is to focus on one task at a time. Important things aren't meant to be done with low focus. They demand your full attention. Let's say you need to do three things. The best approach is to do one thing at a time with complete focus before moving to the second and third tasks. Trying to do all three at once and switching your focus every five minutes may feel productive but it isn't really. It's much better to let your mind get into a flow state as you work on one thing to achieve maximum output. Being constantly distracted will stop you from focusing 1 properly, and your productivity will suffer as a result.

DAILY ROUTINE

"You'll never change your life until you change something you do daily. The secret of your success is found in your daily routine."

— John C. Maxwell

Developing a daily routine is super important. Without one, it will be more difficult for you to be consistent with your work. Some days, you might be motivated and work well; the rest of the days, you might lack motivation and end up procrastinating.

A daily routine can help you to maintain consistency. It can also make you more focused and help you to finish important tasks. Without a routine, it becomes a lot easier to avoid doing anything, or simply opt for the easy tasks and ignore the important ones.

What you do daily is going to shape your future. You are the sum of everything you've done for the past few years. To change who you are, you need to change what you do daily.

A routine is also useful because it helps your mind to stop thinking all the time about what to do next. You can adjust your routine to suit your needs but I suggest you do it right now. Look back at yesterday and see what could have been improved. Now, set that into motion today.

Here is the daily routine of Leo Tolstoy:

Leo Tolstoy was born on 9 September 1828. When he was 18, he started his 'Journal of Daily Activities'. In it, he would write how much time he planned to spend on any task like writing or studying, and then he would later comment on how well he had performed.

He would wake up each day at five o'clock and then take a walk for an hour. He had a strict habit of writing each day. He also slept around 2 hours during the day. He used to work in complete isolation and would go to bed no later than 10 p.m.

His daily routine contributed to his achievements and no one can argue with the fact that he went on to become one of the greatest novelists of his time.

When should you wake up?

You have probably read a ton of advice about what the best time is to wake up. From 4 am to 9 am, everyone has a different opinion on what is the optimum time to rise and shine. It's much more effective to listen to yourself and do what works best for you. Some people thrive on getting up at 5 am, while others need more sleep and find 7 am is a better time for them. Of course, there are a great number of people who would love to stay in bed all day and let life pass them by. The best advice I can give is to set a time that suits you the best– a time that allows you to make the most of each day.

Think for a moment and ask yourself: "What is the best time for me to wake up that will make me more productive and help me achieve my goals?" Don't make the excuse of saying that you should wake up late because you want to be comfortable. You need to choose on behalf of your future self.

Make the right choice, not the easy one.

Sit Alone

"All of humanity's problems stem from our inability to sit quietly in a room alone"

— Blaise Pascal

Have you ever sat down alone to think about what you are doing with your life, what things you're doing that are not improving your life, and instead, making your life worse? If you do this simple daily exercise for 5-10 minutes every day, you will achieve fantastic clarity about your life.

Eliminate All Distractions

The Trojan War was an epic battle between the Greeks and the City of Troy that lasted for ten years. In the end, the Greeks won the war with their famous Trojan Horse. They built a giant wooden horse that was hollow from the inside and left it outside the gates of Troy before the whole army of Greeks left.

The Trojans thought that the Greeks had finally fled, accepting defeat, and had left the horse as a gift. They pulled it inside the City walls, jubilantly celebrating their victory. When night fell, the finest warriors of the Greek army, who were hidden inside the Trojan Horse, sneaked out and opened the gates for their fellow soldier, who had returned, and Troy fell to King Agamemnon and his men.

Think of distractions as being akin to the Trojan Horse. They destroy your focus and distract you from productivity. Be aware of hidden distractions. They can be costly. Even if something distracts you for 2 minutes, 10 minutes are wasted because refocusing takes time.

Delete Apps

We all have apps on our phones and many of them are constant distractions. We spend so much time checking our notifications, browsing our social media pages, and checking in to see what is happening in the world, that the habit is addictive. We find it hard to stop ourselves from being online every minute of the day and waste far too much time in the process.

If you have apps that cause you to be distracted from what you are doing, you can always delete them. In fact, my advice is to delete any app that causes you to lose focus. For many people, it might be games. Once they open the game, they have wasted 15 minutes before even realizing it. I'm not saying that relaxation is bad–everyone needs some downtime–but video games aren't designed for relaxation. They consume a lot of your mental energy, making you even more tired than you were before after playing. There are better ways to relax.

Here's my advice: open your phone and review all the apps and games you waste your time on. Now, delete them. You can always download them again later if you need them.

This simple action will save you from wasting at least 30 minutes every day. Some of you may even save hours!

LEARN TO SAY NO

"Half of the troubles of this life can be traced to saying yes too quickly and not saying no soon enough."

— Josh Billings

If you want to have more control of your life and time, you must learn how to say no when you want to say no. Very often, we say yes, even if we don't want to, simply because we don't want to make the other person sad. You may agree to do everything other people ask of you but you only have a finite amount of energy and time. Saying yes to every opportunity, invite, and task you're asked to do will soon start to feel like a burden. It's perfectly okay to say no when you want to or say yes when you want to. This is the only way to take back your time.

We need to learn how to say no to requests that we have no interest in. This is because if we agree to everything, we will get nothing done. Here is an excellent quote by Steve Jobs:

"People think focus means saying yes to the thing you've got to focus on. But that's not what it means at all. It means saying no to the hundred other good ideas that there are. You have to pick carefully. I'm actually as proud of the things we haven't done as the things I have done. Innovation is saying 'no' to 1,000 things."

DON'T WORK 24/7

"20 years from now, the only people who will remember you worked late are your kids."

— Sahil Bloom

The goal of becoming more productive is not to work more but the opposite. The goal is to get your work done in less time so that you can spend more time with your friends and family. If you work too many hours, then both your creativity and productivity suffer. It's not worth spending 12 hours every day in the office and neglecting all other aspects of your life. Sometimes, it might be necessary, but not all the time.

We should measure productivity by how much work we get done, not by how much time we spend. Unfortunately, many people spend more time in the office than they need to in order to satisfy their egos.

If you're working a lot and still aren't achieving your goals, there is a high chance that you're avoiding the important things that need to be done instead of doing things that aren't that important. The less important things are distracting you from doing the actual important things. This is a form of procrastination and by neglecting the essential things, you won't get the results you want.

I have seen people who do this deliberately. The essential things are hard to do, so instead of doing the hard work, they begin with the easy things that make them appear busy.

Less is More

If you work a lot and are still not able to achieve your goals, there could be two reasons:

1) You may not be working as hard as you think. You may be procrastinating most of the time and not being productive.

2) You may be working on the wrong things. You could be working on less important things, things that don't matter that much. You could be spending most of your time on trivial tasks and don't do the more challenging and essential things.

Everything you do has some value to be gained by doing it. Having said that, some tasks have more value than others in your life. That's why it's so important not to get distracted by less important tasks and, instead, dedicate as much time as possible to the things that matter.

Be Productive, Not Busy

"If the ladder is not leaning against the right wall, every step we take just gets us to the wrong place faster." — Stephen Covey

Working for 12 hours a day doesn't mean anything if you are working on the wrong things. You should work on things that move you toward your goals. There is no use in climbing a ladder and then, halfway up, you look around and realize that you're climbing the wrong ladder. Work on your own dreams, not the dreams of others.

Be productive, not busy. There is no reward for being busy all the time just for the sake of being busy. Instead. Pour your energy into being productive and work on things that move you toward your goals, not away from them.

DON'T WAIT

"Wisdom is knowing what to do next; Skill is knowing how to do it, and Virtue is doing it."

— David Starr Jordan

The one main reason that a lot of people underachieve is that they're always waiting for the right time to do something but guess what? The right time never comes and there's no time like the present. You can either start today and make some progress, or you can wait and console yourself that your time will come.

You need to throw out this idea that, eventually, your time will come without putting in the work. It just won't happen. To achieve any of your goals, you need to do the hard work. I have seen zero successful people who are still waiting for the perfect time.

Yes, some goals take time to come to fruition and, no matter how you try, can't be realized any faster. But that doesn't mean that you shouldn't try in the first place and sit around waiting for a miracle to happen.

Don't confuse laziness with patience–both are very different concepts. As long as you put the work in every day, having patience will benefit you until you achieve the results you want.

A Story of Great Patience

A farmer once planted a bamboo tree. He watered the sapling daily for a year but saw no sign of life. No growth, no sprouts, no hope. The second year was the same, and the third and fourth after that. His patience and faith in this "miracle" bamboo plant soon faded although he continued to water it daily anyway. During the fifth year, just as he was about to give up on his dream of growing the tree he noticed it was beginning to sprout. Much to his delight, the bamboo sprung up 60 feet over the next six weeks!

This is an excellent story about both patience and hard work. Life is just the same. Success rarely comes overnight and it takes a long time to happen, although that doesn't mean you should sit around doing nothing. The crop didn't grow independently; the farmer had to plant it, take care of it, and be patient.

Impatient With Action and Patient with Results

A student of Zen went to his teacher and asked earnestly, "I am devoted to studying Zen. How long will it take me to master it?"

"Ten years," the teacher said.

Impatiently, the student answered, "But I want to master it faster than that. I will work very hard. I will practice every day for ten or more hours if necessary. How long will it take then?"

The teacher thought for a moment before replying, "20 years."

You see, you have no control over what results you will get in life. You can only control your actions and the work you do. Everyone wants to get fast results when they're working hard, thinking they should be rewarded right now for their work. But generally speaking, that doesn't happen. You may work hard for years before you get the results you want so need to be patient. That doesn't mean you should be patient about taking action. Don't be one of those people who thinks everything will come to them automatically. You must do the work first before you get the results you want.

"A man who is a master of patience is master of everything else." — George Savile

No Perfect Time

There is no such thing as perfect timing to start anything new. Start today and make some progress or keep waiting for the ideal time, which will never come. The perfect time is actually now. There is no better time than today to start moving toward your goals. Stop being lazy and start doing the work that is required.

Consistency Is Key

Picasso was walking through the market in Paris when a woman approached him.

She pulled out a piece of paper and said, “Mr. Picasso, I am a fan of your work. Please, could you do a little drawing for me?”

Picasso smiled and quickly drew a piece of art on the paper. He handed it back to her.

“That will be one million francs.”

The lady was shocked. “How can you ask for so much? It took you five minutes to draw this!”

“No,” Picasso replied. “It took me 40 years to draw this in five minutes.”

To be great at anything, you must do it daily and for a long time.

- To become a better painter, you need to paint every day.

- To become a better writer, you need to write every day.
- To become a better speaker, you need to speak every day.

Most people never start; some start but give up as soon as things get complicated; only a few are consistent and show up every day, no matter how hard it gets.

It Will Get Easy

"It may seem difficult at first, but everything is difficult at first." — Miyamoto Musashi

The hardest thing is to start. That's where 95% of people get stuck. They never start and keep making excuses. If you want to break a bad habit, the first few days will be the hardest but after a few weeks, it will get pretty easy to keep going.

Do What You Say

If you love to procrastinate, you will not honor your words. If you say that you're going to do something and then you don't do it, people will soon stop trusting you. I'm not implying that you do everything other people ask you to do but when you finally say that you're going to do something, then you better do it. If you say that from tomorrow you're going to go to the gym every day, you better go to the gym, no matter what happens. Do what you say and honor your word–you will feel so good about yourself if you do!

DON'T WORRY

"I am an old man and have known many troubles, most of which never happened."

— Mark Twain

Worrying loves a lazy person because lazy people have nothing else to do except worry. Since they aren't doing any work, all they can do is worry about the future. If you believe in yourself, then there is no need to worry. When you don't believe in yourself, the worry starts to appear. All types of negative thoughts begin to enter your mind and you start worrying about things that are very unlikely to happen.

Worrying can only be destroyed by one thing, and that is through action.

That's the only way I know to make your worries go away. I have no other wisdom to give you. Let's say you're worried about your health. The only thing you can do is to start taking care of your health. There is nothing else you can do. Thinking about your health all day will not make you healthier; it might even do the opposite.

It's normal to worry about some things. We all worry about our jobs, businesses, health, money, family, etc. The trick is to classify your worries into two categories:

1) The things that you can control and you can do something about.
2) The things you can't control and you can't do anything about.

Worrying about the first category is okay. You have to worry about your health so that you can take some action and improve it. This is what I call good worrying. It helps you do things that can make your life better.

Worrying about the second part is stupid. Why worry about something you can't control? Let's say that tomorrow, an asteroid is coming to Earth and going to kill all of us. What's the worry? You can't do anything about it. Worrying about things you can't control is going to rob you of your happiness.

Make a new rule to never worry again about anything that you can't control and, if you can control it, then act immediately and do something about it. In both cases, there should be no worry.

DELEGATE

If you want to do a few small things right, do them yourself. Learn to delegate if you want to do great things and make a big impact.

— John C. Maxwell

There is no way that you can do everything by yourself. No matter what technique, hack, or tips you try, there will never be enough time to do everything alone and that's a good thing because we don't need to do everything by ourselves. Other people can help us to do the things we don't have time for.

If you have a task that needs to be done and no time to do it, it's a low-value task. This means that even if you don't do it by yourself and hire someone else instead it won't make a difference.

Many things that may take a lot of your time that aren't that important. You can delegate them right now so you can use the time to do the things you want to do.

Make a list of all the non-important tasks you need to do every day, how much time it takes to do them, and how much money it will take for someone else to do them. You will see that you're doing things that can be easily outsourced very cheaply and that take up a lot of your time daily. Try this for a few things and then see how it goes.

Even if somebody else does around 90% of a good job, it's worth it. Also, there is a high chance that somebody else will do a better job than you. You think that you can do a better job but that's not always true. You may, for example, think you are an expert at washing your car, but a professional car wash service will give much better results!

HOW TO LEARN ANYTHING FASTER

"I constantly see people rise in life who are not the smartest, sometimes not even the most diligent, but they are learning machines."

— Charlie Munger

Learn What Is Useful

Don't learn anything just for the sake of learning it. Focus instead on learning things that can improve your life. Rather than spending time learning some obscure language that no one speaks anymore (unless you are an archaeologist or anthropologist!) learn Spanish or Chinese! In other words, think about what is useful to you or not. If not, don't spend time learning it. There are thousands of other things you can learn today that are beneficial and will improve your life.

No Laziness While Learning

You can't be lazy if you're trying to learn something. Have to jump into action and begin learning now. Let's say you want to learn how to code. Start right now–what are you waiting for? Speed is crucial. I'm not saying to watch videos at 3x but you should have a sense of urgency. Learn at whatever pace you're comfortable with, but start it now. You will thank yourself later.

Speed Reading

"If you can speed read it, it isn't worth reading."

— Naval Ravikant

I'm not a huge fan of speed-reading books, as great books worth reading demand your complete attention. The fastest way to read more books is to spend more time on books. That's it. There are some books I spent weeks on and some that I even read in a day. Don't think too much about reading speeds. If you're a beginner, it will get better over time. Focus more on the quality of the books you read. Also, it's a good idea to increase the variety of books you would normally read. This helps you to expand, grow, and gain greater knowledge. Don't stick to the same type of books just because you are used to them.

- Read fiction.
- Read non-fiction.
- Read self-help.
- Read history.
- Read philosophy.
- Read biographies.
- Read Autobiographies.

Read everything.

DISSS Method

This method was created by Tim Ferriss to learn anything fast. It stands for "Deconstruction, Selection, Sequencing, Stakes, and Speed."

Here is how to use this method:

• Deconstruction: Break down the skill you want to learn into small parts. Find out the most important part, which is the building block of the skill.

• Selection: Use the 80/20 Rule. Focus on the top 20% part which is most important. It will help you in learning around 80% of the skill.

• Sequencing: Find the most effective way to learn. Start with the easy part first and then move on to more complex parts.

• Stakes: Add some stakes to keep yourself motivated and disciplined. Tell your friends and family about your goals. Keep yourself accountable.

5 Hour Rule

This rule is simple: no matter how busy or how tired you are each day, spend at least 1 hour trying to learn something new. You would do this for 5 days in a week. As Charlie Munger said,

"Those who keep learning, will keep rising in life."

Apply What You Learn

Warren Buffett read *"How to Win Friends and Influence People"* by Dale Carnegie when he was only 9 years old. Most people would read a book and then keep doing what they've been doing previously but not him. He decided to test whether the book's principle would work or not so he started testing it on other people. To one group he would give attention and show appreciation and to another group, he would disagree with them. He ran this experiment and kept track of the results.

Once it was proven that it worked, he adopted it into his life.

That's how things are done. Don't just read, do tests to figure out whether it works or not and then apply it in your own life.

Part 2

Tips & Techniques

"The tragedy in life doesn't lie in not reaching your goal. The tragedy lies in having no goal to reach." — Benjamin E. Mays

PYGMALION EFFECT

In the late 19th century, Wilhelm Von Osten had a horse that he claimed could add, subtract, multiply, or divide. The questions could be asked orally or in writing and the horse would answer them by tapping its foot. The horse's accuracy was around 90 percent, which was an astonishing feat. Everyone was amazed at how the horse could do this. Many people thought it was some kind of trick but it wasn't. The horse answered correctly even when the question was asked by other people.

In 1907, the psychologist Oskar Pfungst found out how the horse was doing it. When a person was behind the screen or didn't know the answer themselves, the horse's answers were mostly incorrect. The horse was reading human body language. When a question was asked, it would start tapping and when it reached the correct answer, the questioner would give non-verbal cues such as tilting their head or clapping. The horse would recognize these cues and stop.

The reason why the horse could answer the questions correctly is because people had expectations that he would answer correctly. It's the same when it comes to our achievements. If you have high expectations of yourself in any given area, you're more likely to perform better. This is known as the Pygmalion Effect. If you consider yourself a hard-working person, you will work harder. The opposite of this is known as the Golem Effect. If you consider yourself to be a lazy person, you're more likely to procrastinate. Simple!

20 PRODUCTIVITY TIPS I WISH I HAD KNOWN EARLIER

1) Plan your day.
2) Write everything you want to achieve in a day.
3) Write your goals on a physical paper.
4) Follow the 80/20 Rule. 20% of your work will bring you 80% of your results.
5) Stop Multitasking. Switching tasks significantly reduces your productivity.
6) Focus on one task at a time.
7) Remove all distractions from your environment.
8) When tired, take a nap.
9) Learn to say no. You will never have enough time if you say yes to everything.
10) Delegate all the non-important tasks.
11) Don't wait for the perfect time. Do It Now.

12) Anything that can be done in under five minutes should be done now.
13) Do the task that you hate first.
14) Set deadlines; the task will never be finished without deadlines.
15) Stop focusing on things that don't help you achieve your goals.
16) Don't be a perfectionist when it's not required.
17) Schedule a time when you're going to check your email.
18) Avoid all unnecessary meetings.
19) Avoid negative people at all costs.
20) Do what you love.

80/20 RULE

This is also called the Pareto Principle. It basically means that 20% of your work will bring you 80% of the results.

There are many things you can do each day but there are a few things that are important and will bring the most results, and there are other things less important that will not help us achieve our goals.

Even if you don't procrastinate, you should still be very aware of what you're doing because if you're doing things that aren't valuable and won't help you achieve your goals, you're wasting your time.

Think for a moment. What is the most important thing you can do to help you achieve your goals?

8 JAPANESE TECHNIQUES TO OVERCOME LAZINESS

1. IKIGAI

This means to have a purpose in life. It's the reason you wake up each morning, excited to do something. When you have a purpose, you won't feel lazy or unmotivated.

The Four Rules of IKIGAI are:

1) Do what you love
2) Do what you're good at
3) Do what the world needs
4) Do what you can be paid for

2. Kaizen

Kaizen means focusing on small improvements every day instead of waiting for big improvements. It's about trying to become 1% better every day. Instead of setting a big goal, divide it into multiple small goals and tackle each of them one by one.

3. Shoshin

This is another interesting concept taken from Zen Buddhism. It means approaching things with a beginner's mindset.

"If your mind is empty ... It is open to everything. In the beginner's mind, there are many possibilities, but in the expert's mind, there are few."
— Shunryu Suzuki (author of Zen Mind, Beginner's Mind)

4. Hara Hachi Bu

This means to stop eating after you're 80% full. If you eat too much, you're more likely to feel lazy. This happens to people all the time. Once they eat their lunch, they start to feel tired because the body tries to digest all the food they ate. They start to feel sleepy, and have no energy to work, preferring to procrastinate until they feel more alert.

5. Shinrin-yoku

Shinrin in Japanese means "forest," and yoku means "bath."

This simple philosophy implies that one should spend more time in nature. Spending time in natural surroundings is the best way to deal with stress so, whenever things are getting on top of you or you feel overwhelmed, go for a walk in nature.

6. Wabi-sabi

This concept states that, instead of perfection, one should find beauty in imperfection. Things can't be perfect all the time. Some things just can't be perfect, and that's okay. There is beauty even in perfection.

Love things the way they are. Don’t be stubborn and try to change them. You will ruin their beauty.

7. Ganbaru

Ganbaru is a Japanese term meaning "doing one's best" or "persevering." It emphasizes giving maximum effort and persisting through challenges with determination and resilience. Basically, adopt a mindset of continuous improvement and the belief that success is attainable through persistent effort and commitment.

8. Gaman

This concept means to show patience and perseverance when things get too hard. When you go on a journey it’s not going to be all pleasant. There will be a lot of times when things will go wrong. You will face many difficulties when you start doing the things you want to do. There will be failures.

10 TINY HABITS THAT WILL CHANGE YOUR LIFE

1. Move Your Body

Our bodies are not made to sit all day. If you don't do any physical work, then you will feel tired all the time. Move your body every day, no matter whether it's physical work or some sort of exercise. Go for a run early in the morning or when you feel overwhelmed during work, go for a walk.

2. You Are What You Eat

What you eat will impact the way you feel during the day. If you feel lethargic, then maybe you need to change what you eat. It depends on person to person, so look at your diet and see whether you can improve it.

3. Have A Purpose

If you have no purpose, you will never have the energy to do anything. If you don't love your job, you won't be excited about it or filled with energy. You need to have a sense of purpose to have constant motivation to work hard. Find a purpose in your life.

4. Drink More Water

Make sure that you're drinking plenty of water throughout the day.

5. Surround Yourself with People You Love

Be around people you love and care about–people who make you feel happy and blissful. Stop surrounding yourself with negative people and move away from those full of toxicity.

6. Take Risks

If you're not taking risks, then you will not have the motivation to do things. Our mind needs constant challenges to keep it alert, and if you're doing the same task over and over, then your motivation will decrease.

7. Don't Overload Yourself

Stop having unrealistic expectations of yourself. You need to push yourself but if you do it too much, it will have a negative effect. Stop trying to do too many things in a day and stick to a few important ones.

8. Don't Try to Multitask

Multitasking is overrated. It quickly exhausts you and doesn't allow you to focus on any one task. It's more of a distraction than a useful skill. Switching tasks reduces your productivity instead of boosting it. Simply don't multitask.

9. Eliminating All Distractions

The best thing you can do is to eliminate all the distractions from your environment. Anything that diverts your brain's energy should be eliminated.

10. Having a Sense of Urgency

You can't achieve anything in your life if you don't have a sense of urgency. You need to be patient with results and impatient with action. Anything you need to do should be done as fast as possible.

POMODORO TECHNIQUE

This technique is very simple. What you need to do is work for 25 minutes uninterrupted, then take a break for 5 minutes, and then repeat.

I like to go for a long time before taking a break. You must see for yourself when you're tired and then adjust this technique accordingly. Rest is very important and during your working day, you should take a break whenever you feel you're mentally tired after working for long periods or working intensively.

If you're fully engrossed in any task, you may have noticed that you stop worrying about everything else; you even stop noticing the passage of time. This may not happen often, but when it does, you feel happy. This joy can only happen if you're doing something that you love. You can't experience this if you don't like your job. Loving what you do is the only way to feel this.

5 Minute Rule

You always have a list of tasks to do because you tend to procrastinate even about small tasks that can be done instantly or in under 5 minutes. These are the ones you keep putting off until later. In reality, you never get around to them and the to-do list just keeps getting larger and larger. By now, you feel overwhelmed by the substantial number of pending tasks that need to be done.

In the end, you get nothing done because doing one or two things will not be enough to clear the backlog. A new rule you should always apply is to do whatever can be done in under 5 minutes now. Don't put it off until tomorrow. Just do it now.

As Benjamin Franklin said:

"Beware of little expenses - a small leak will sink a great ship."

In the same way, we should beware of all the little things we have to do as they will destroy our productivity.

TWO DAY RULE

I saw a YouTube video by Matt D'Avella about this rule a year ago and it's the simplest and yet most effective way to be consistent with your habits.

Every year, we make resolutions in January to improve our lives and to build better habits. Just 15 days later, we start doing the same things we were doing before the new year. Do one thing next year: go to the gym on 1 January and you will see this for yourself. The gym is packed and then, with each passing day, fewer and fewer people turn up. You might miss a few days in a row and after that, you lose the drive to go anymore. The time you would have dedicated to going to the gym is now taken up by some other activity.

The two-day rule is simple: do not miss anything for two days straight. You can miss something for one day if you have to but never for two days.

New habits take time to form and the early days are the hardest. That's when there is a high chance you will quit and go back to your usual habits. If you can overcome the early days urge to quit, then it becomes much easier to keep moving.

Every person is the sum of all their good and bad habits and there is a constant battle between the two. If you don't form good habits, the bad ones take over. The thing is, most good habits are meant to be hard because that's how they hold their value. It's the hard part in anything that makes the difference.

Learning a new skill is hard, going to the gym every day is hard. The fact that very few people do these things is the reason that these things are appreciated. If the same things were done by everyone then it would be the new normal. You doing a different thing than anybody else makes it valuable and rewarding. As Muhammad Ali said,

"I hated every minute of training but I said, 'Don't quit. Suffer now and live the rest of your life as a champion.'"

WAKE UP!

"When you arise in the morning, think of what a precious privilege it is to be alive, to breathe, to think, to enjoy, to love." — Marcus Aurelius

The time for you to do the things that you want to do is running out. Soon, you will be filled with the regret of not doing the things you wanted to do. When those regrets arise, there isn't much you can do except feel angry at yourself and wish you had done things differently. Now is the time to do it.

Whatever it is you want to do: spending more time with your family, traveling around the world, or focusing on your health, now is the time.

You must always live with a sense of urgency. We have a very short lifespan. I don't want to make you feel sad or anxious but gently remind you of that fact.

Wake up and start doing things differently. You will get the same results if you stay at your current job. You must change what you do to change the results you want.

The life you want to live is on the other side of laziness. Living each day with complete awareness, enjoying each moment, and living not in the future or past but in the present. Your future can only be changed by the things you do in the present.

- Each day is important.
- Each hour is important.
- Each moment is important.

Don't live your life according to the expectations of other people. You will always regret that in the future. Why listen to other people and not listen to your inner voice, which is trying to guide you to the right path?

If you're a 30-year-old and you're going to live up to the age of 90, you have already spent 1/3rd of your life. If you're happy with the way you spent your previous day, then great! But if you don’t like your past you must do whatever it takes so by the time you are 70, you won’t say, "I have wasted my entire life."

Drop everything holding you back from living your life the way you want. Don’t worry about other people's opinions. Their unhappiness has nothing to do with you. If they are filled with regrets and want you to have the same kind of regrets, don't let them influence you.

Once, a father and a son were coming back from a village far away, where they had purchased a donkey. They overheard a man saying, “See the fools. They have a donkey but are still walking on foot.” The man and his son thought it was a good idea so they sat on the donkey.

On their way, another villager saw them and said, “Look at the poor donkey. He can hardly walk.” The man felt sorry for the donkey and got off. While crossing the fields, a woman remarked, “Your son is young and healthy. He should walk and let you sit on the donkey.” The son then told his father, “I am sorry, Dad. Please come and sit on the donkey,” so they changed places.

As they were about to reach their village, a passerby commented, “Hey, see the selfish man; his poor son is walking while he’s enjoying the ride."

Without giving another thought, both the son and father tied the donkey upside down to a long bamboo and carried it through the village.

By the time they reached home, everyone was laughing at them. A village elder asked, “Why are you carrying this donkey like this? Can’t it walk?”

The father explained what had happened on the way and the old man replied, "Everyone was laughing at you because instead of using your senses, you kept on doing what others said."

One day, just like this book, your life will end. Do the things you want to do now. Travel to the places you want to. Read the books you want to.

Surround yourself with the people you want to.

Time is running out. Start living.

NOTES

- Andrei, V. (n.d.). Retrieved from The Sovereign Artist: https://vizi.substack.com/
- Aurelius, M. (n.d.). *Meditations.* Modern Library.
- Bezos, J. (n.d.). *2016 Letter to Shareholders.* Retrieved from Amazon: https://www.aboutamazon.com/news/company-news/2016-letter-to-shareholders
- Billings, J. (2023). *The Complete Works of Josh Billings.* Good Press.
- Bloom, S. (2023, March 3). Retrieved from X: https://twitter.com/SahilBloom/status/1631281464313610246?
- Bloom, S. (2023, May 17). Retrieved from X: https://twitter.com/SahilBloom/status/1658809456375857153?
- Churchill, W. (1943, September 6). *Winston Churchill's Honorary Degree Speech.* Retrieved from Harvard Magazine:

- https://www.harvardmagazine.com/2018/09/churchill-harvard-september-6-1943
- Epictetus. (2008). *Discourses and Selected Writings.* Penguin Publishing Group.
- Franklin, B. (1757). *The Way to Wealth.*
- Fuggle, L. (2023, September 23). *Tolstoy's 'Rules of Life,' Perfectionism and Constant Self-Improvement.* Retrieved from Tolstoy Therapy: https://tolstoytherapy.com/tolstoys-rules-and-perfectionism/
- Hormozi, A. (2023, June 19). Retrieved from X: https://twitter.com/AlexHormozi/status/1670518034006507522
- Isaacson, W. (2011). *Steve Jobs.* Thorndike Press.
- Isaacson, W. (2017). *Leonardo Da Vinci.* Simon and Schuster.
- Jobs, S. (2005, June 12). *Steve Jobs' 2005 Stanford Commencement Address.* Retrieved from YouTube: https://www.youtube.com/watch?v=UF8uR6Z6KLc

- Koch, R. (1999). *The 80/20 Principle, Expanded and Updated: The Secret to Achieving More with Less.* Crown.
- Life, T. A. (2011). *Tolstoy: A Russian Life.* Houghton Mifflin Harcourt.
- Musashi, M. (n.d.). *The Book of Five Rings.*
- Orbiter, M. C. (1999). *Mars Climate Orbiter.* Retrieved from NASA: https://science.nasa.gov/mission/mars-climate-orbiter/
- Parrish, S. (2020, June 29). Retrieved from X: https://twitter.com/shaneaparrish/status/1277415631965519873
- Progress, P. L. (1986). *Parkinson's Law.* Penguin.
- Rohn, J. (n.d.).
- Seneca. (2004). *Letters from a Stoic.* Penguin Books.
- Steven Naifeh, G. W. (2012). *Van Gogh: The Life.* Random House Publishing Group.
- Zuckerberg, M. (2011). Interview with Mark Zuckerberg at Startup School in 2011.

- Avella, M. D. (2019, September). *Two Day Rule*. From YouTube: https://www.youtube.com/watch?v=bfLHTLQZ5nc&t=327s&pp=ygUMdHdvIGRheSBydWxl

- *https://thedecisionlab.com/biases/the-pygmalion-effect*. (n.d.). Retrieved from The Decision Lab: https://thedecisionlab.com/biases/the-pygmalion-effect

www.ingramcontent.com/pod-product-compliance
Lightning Source LLC
Chambersburg PA
CBHW031600060326
40783CB00026B/4158
9798870369396